RUBANK EDUCATIONAL LIBRAR

RUBANK Elementary METHOD

STRING BASS

SYLVAN D. WARD

A FUNDAMENTAL COURSE FOR INDIVIDUAL OR LIKE-INSTRUMENT CLASS INSTRUCTION

RUBANK®

HAL•LEONARD® CORPORATION
7777 W. BLUEMOUND RD. P.O. BOX 13819 MILWAUKEE, WI 53213

Illustration 1

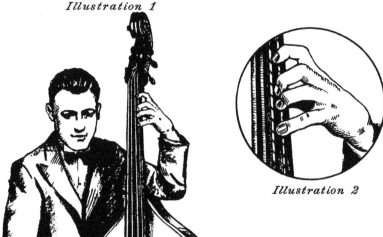

Illustration 2

The instrument reclines slightly toward the player and is steadied by the left thigh and knee.

The ball of the left thumb rests directly under the neck of the instrument, opposite the second finger. Place the fingers firmly on the string as shown in Illustration 2.

Stand straight. Do not stoop over bass. The right arm should hang naturally from the shoulder and should not be crooked at the elbow.

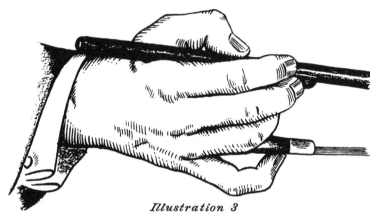

Illustration 3

There are two different types of bows — the German model and the French model. The Illustration above shows the German model which is the one in most common use.

(a) The thumb rests on top of the bow. The first and second fingers are extended close together along side of the stick. The third finger is curved toward the palm. The fourth finger may be held inside of the frog next to the third finger, or it may be placed on the outside as shown in Illustration 3.

(b) The hand and fingers should feel relaxed with the frog of the bow resting at the base of the fingers, and never clutched or gripped in the palm of the hand.

(c) The French model bow (not illustrated here) is shaped like a cello bow and is held similarly. See Rubank Elementary Cello Method.

HOW TO TUNE

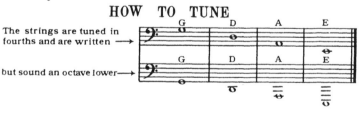

The strings are tuned in fourths and are written →

but sound an octave lower →

Illustration 4

HOLDING THE BOW FOR PIZZICATO PLAYING

Hold the bow with the third and fourth fingers as shown in Illustration 4 and pluck the string with the first finger. (Some symphony players pluck with both the first and second fingers to provide necessary strength.) The thumb is placed against the edge of the fingerboard.

Because of the depth of the tones, it is sometimes difficult to hear the strings clearly when tuning. Therefore, it is advisable to make the string sound an octave higher. You can do this by placing the third finger of the left hand lightly on the string at its half way point.

A comprehensive Chart showing notes and fingerings in all positions is on pages 62 and 63.

Learning To Bow On The Open Strings

The exercises on this page are to enable you to get the "feel" of the bow, and draw it straight (parallel with the bridge). Note values and counting will be taken up on the next page.

OPEN STRINGS
E A D G

← Nut

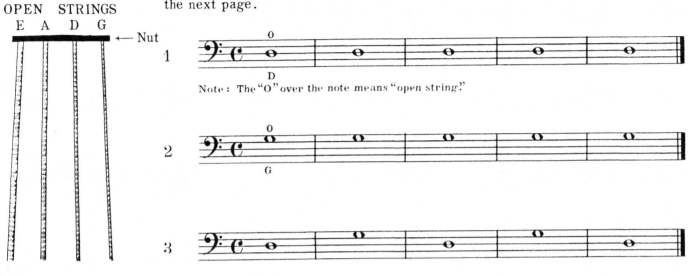

Note: The "O" over the note means "open string."

Check up on your playing position.
Are you bowing correctly? Refer to illustration, page 2.

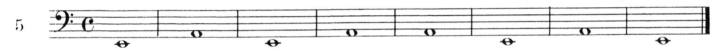

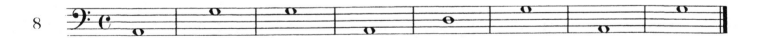

Half Notes and Half Rests

Half Position

Learning the notes and fingering on the G string

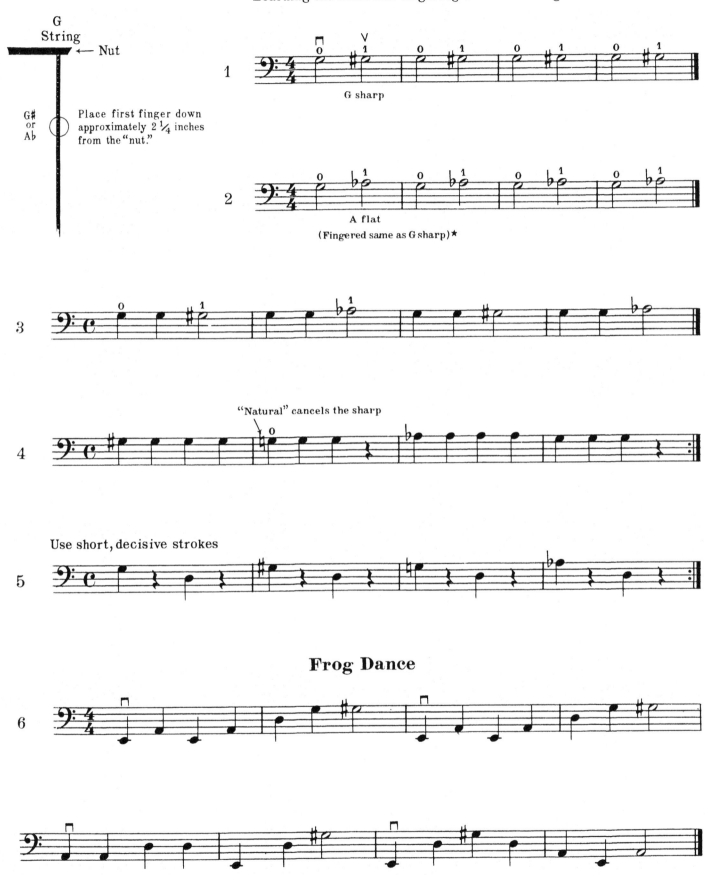

Frog Dance

*Notes such as A♭ and G♯ which sound the same but are notated differently on the staff are called "enharmonic tones."

Learning To Use The Second Finger

Make sure that your left hand is in the correct playing position. Study illustration page 2.

When you play the second finger you also place the first finger down in its proper position.

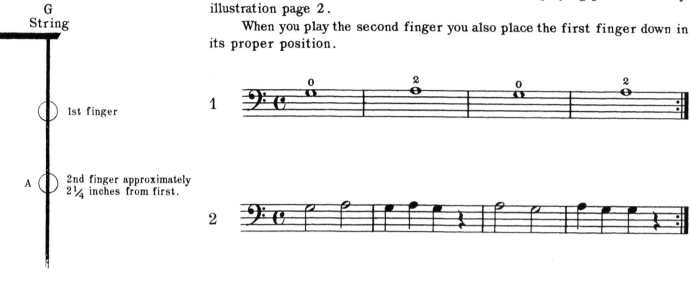

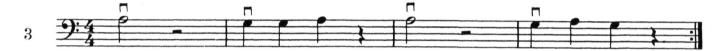

3/4 Time

3/4 Time. Three beats to a measure and each quarter note gets one beat.

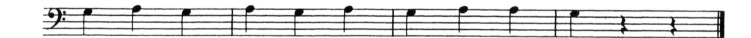

A Familiar Bass Part

Learning To Use The Fourth Finger

When you play the fourth finger you also place the other fingers down in their proper position.

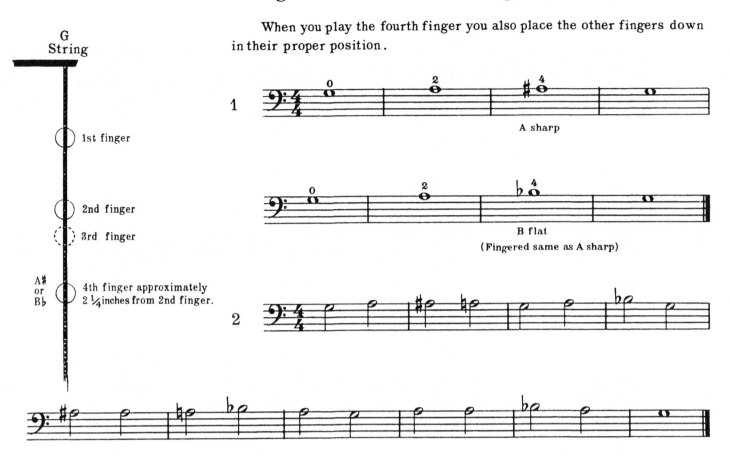

A sharp

B flat
(Fingered same as A sharp)

Dotted Half Notes

A dot after a note increases the value of the note one half.

Name the notes before playing them.

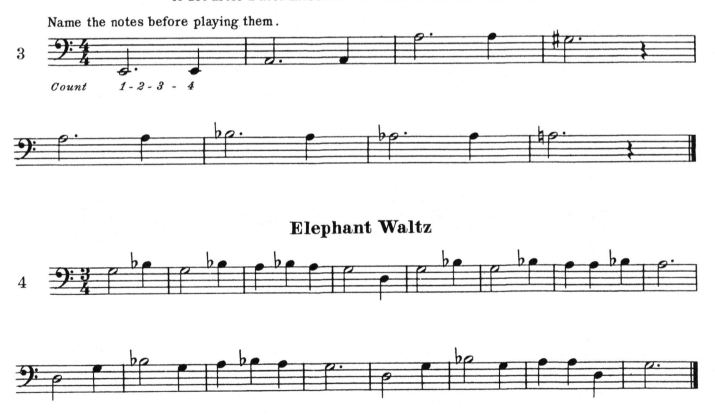

Count   1 - 2 - 3 - 4

Elephant Waltz

8

Bass Part to a Waltz

March in 2/4 Time

2/4 Time. Two beats to a measure and each quarter note gets one beat.

Count   1   2   1   2

The Tie

Are you counting evenly?

"Tie"–Play both notes in one bow

Leap Frog

S. D. W.

39587

Playing on the D String

Finger distance same as on G string

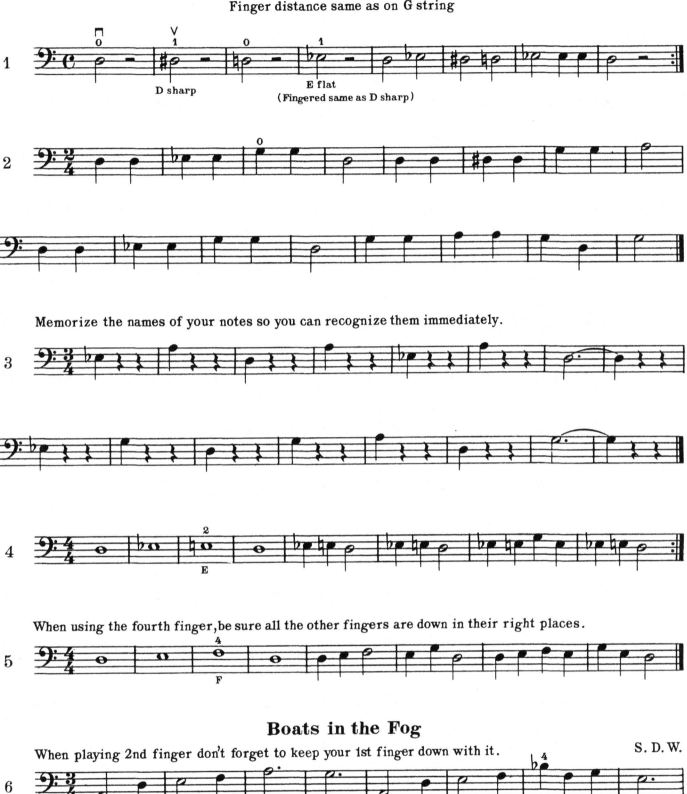

1 D sharp
E flat
(Fingered same as D sharp)

2

Memorize the names of your notes so you can recognize them immediately.

3

4 E

When using the fourth finger, be sure all the other fingers are down in their right places.

5 F

Boats in the Fog

When playing 2nd finger don't forget to keep your 1st finger down with it.

S. D. W.

6

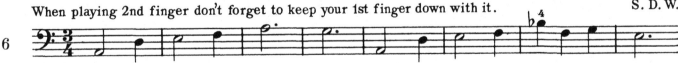

Up and Down

Dunce Dance

S. D. W.

Count the rests carefully.

Across the Strings

Strive to produce nice clear tones. Listen to each one to make sure it is right.

Playing on the A String

A sharp

B flat
(Fingered same as A sharp)

Name the notes before playing them.

B

C

Andante

S. D. W.

Play with full tone.

Finger Play

Etude

S.D.W

The Slur

Playing two or more notes in one bow

Cavalry March

Play short, quick strokes

Playing on the E String

Little Waltz

Playing F Sharp and G Flat

Playing G♮

Familiar Melody

Song of the Tumbleweed

S. D. W.

Eighth Notes

Dotted Quarter Notes

Solo

German Folk Song

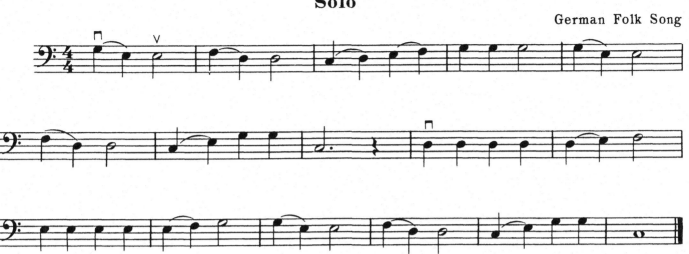

F Major and B Flat Major Scales

F Major and B♭ Major are natural half position keys and if the student keeps this in mind there will be less unnecessary shifting out of position when playing pieces in these keys.

F MAJOR

Notice that B flat has been put here (in the signature) which means that all B's will be flatted unless other-wise indicated.

B♭ MAJOR

Notice that E flat has been added to the signature which means that all E's will be flatted unless other-wise indicated.

Prairie Song

S. D. W.

Notice that all B's and E's are to be flatted in this piece.

Variations on the F Major Scale

Variations on the B♭ Major Scale

Practice different bowings.

Alla Breve Time

Alla Breve – Quickens the time. Means each half note gets one beat.

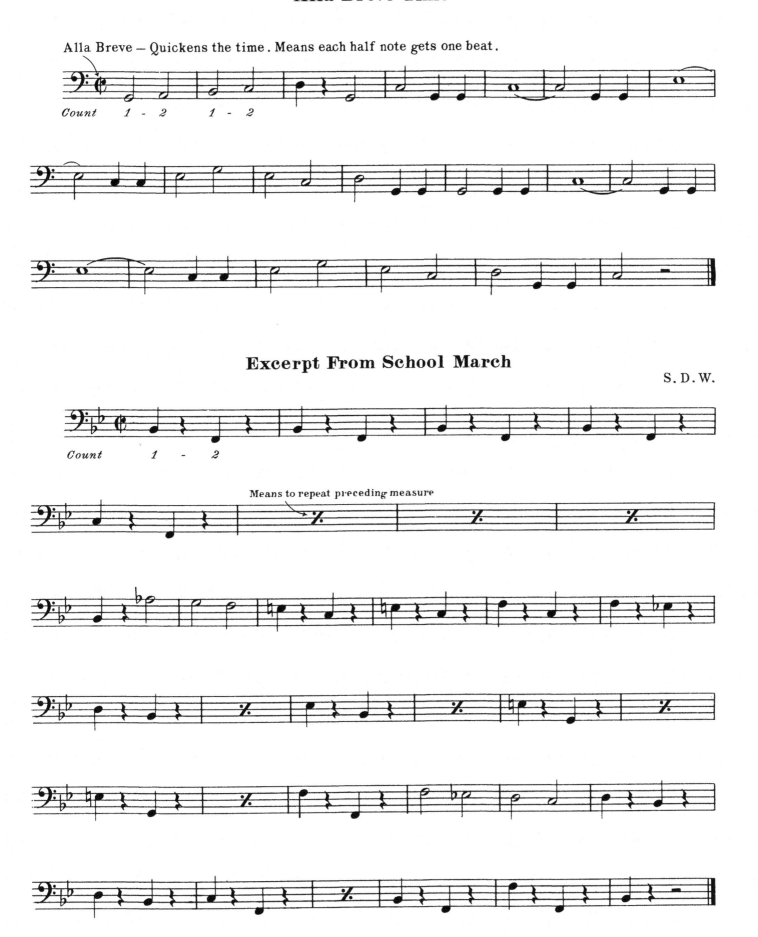

Excerpt From School March

S. D. W.

Means to repeat preceding measure

18

Reuben and Rachel

At Pierrot's Door

French Folk Song

Orchestra Bass Part to Above Melody

19

Part of C Major Scale Playable in Half Position

Notice there are no flats or sharps in the key of C Major.

Half step

Do Re Mi Fa So Fa Mi Re Do

6/8 Time

Clap hands with rhythm before playing, slightly accenting the 1st and 4th notes.

6/8 Time. Six beats to a measure and each eighth note gets one beat.

Count   1 - 2 - 3 - 4 - 5 - 6
or   1   -   2

Familiar Melody

Clap rhythm before playing.

Count   1 - 2 - 3 - 4 - 5 - 6
or   1   -   2

America

Orchestra String Bass Part

39587

Part of E♭ Major Scale Playable in Half Position

Notice there are 3 flats in the key of E♭ Major. Name them in their order.

Melodious Etude

S. D. W.

Crossing the Strings

First Position

In order to increase the range of notes it is necessary to learn various positions. This book proceeds with the first, second, third and fourth positions including the intermediate positions. In shifting from half to first position, merely slide the thumb and fingers quickly along the neck of the instrument. (See reference chart of all positions on page 62 and 63.)

When using 4th finger, keep all fingers down.

Melody

S. D. W.

First Position on the D String

Jumping Around

Stomping Bass

Notice that F# and C# have been put in the signature, which means that these notes are to be sharped throughout the piece unless cancelled by a "Natural" sign.(♮)

S. D. W.

Learning Detached Bowing

Etude

First Position on the A String

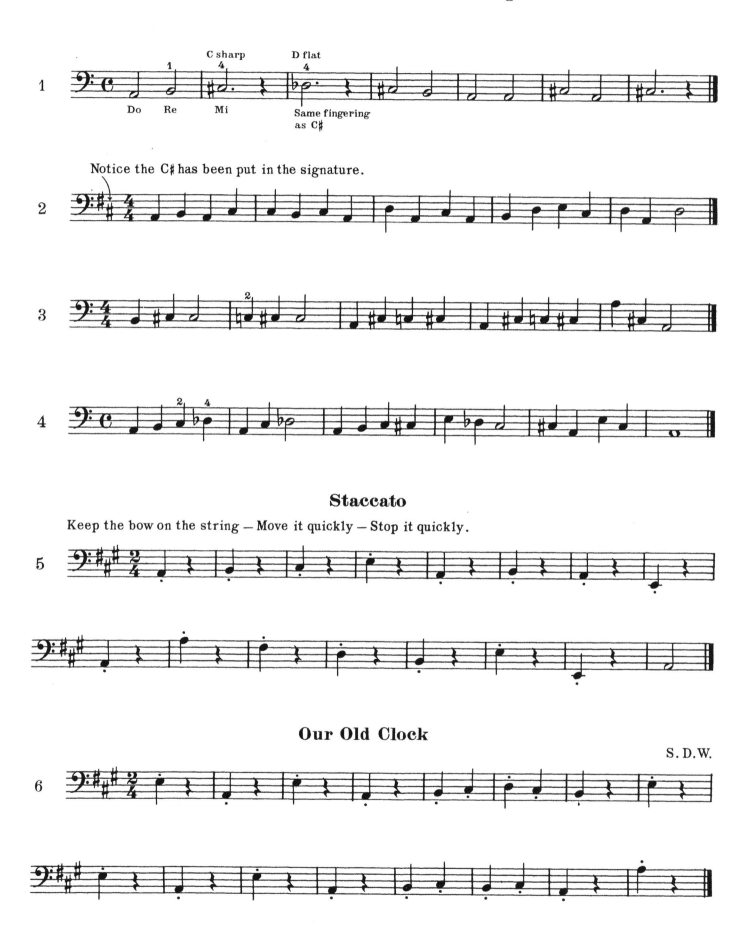

Staccato

Keep the bow on the string — Move it quickly — Stop it quickly.

Our Old Clock

S. D. W.

First Position on the E String

Notice the signature so you will be sure to observe what notes are to be sharped in this exercise.

Camel Ride

S. D. W.

Crossing the Strings in First Position

Scales That Are Playable in First Position

G Major is a natural first position key. Keep this in mind when playing pieces in this key, so as to avoid unnecessary shifting back and forth from one position to another.

G MAJOR Notice there is one sharp in the key of G Major, and the name of it is F♯.

Half step

Half step

We Three Kings of Orient Are
(Orchestra Bass Part)

JOHN H. HOPKINS

3/8 Time — Three beats to the measure and each eighth note gets one beat.

Count   1   2   3

Part of D Major Scale Playable in 1st Position

Notice there are 2 sharps in the key of D Major — F♯ and C♯.

Melody in D Major

Shifting Between Half and First Positions

In making the shift, the hand, fingers and thumb move as one unit.
Practice carefully

Chromatic Scale

Name the notes before playing them.

A Major Scale Playable in First and Half Positions

There are 3 sharps in the key of A Major. Memorize so you won't forget.

Variation on the A Major Scale

Practice different bowings.

Make it a rule to shift as few times as possible.

Singing Strings

S. D. W.

March
Orchestra Bass Part

E Major Scale Playable in First and Half Positions

4 sharps in the key of E Major.

March Captain

Listen carefully to play in tune.

B Major Scale Played in First and Half Position

Notice there are 5 sharps in the key of B Major. Name them in their order.

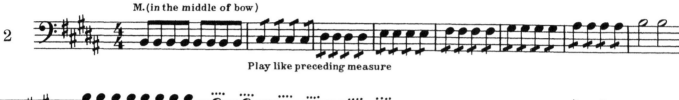

Wrist Bowing

M.(in the middle of bow)

Play like preceding measure

Play like preceding measure

Bowing in Style

Use fingerings as marked for practice.

Like preceding measure.

A♭ Major Scale and Part of D♭ Major Scale Played in 1st and Half Positions

Preliminary Exercise

A♭ Major Scale

Notice there are 4 flats in this key. Name them.

D♭ Major Scale

There are 5 flats in this key. Name them.

Melody in A♭ Major

S. D. W.

Sixteenth Notes

Grasshopper Hop

Practice slowly in the middle of the bow, then increase tempo.

Allegro

S. D. W.

Count   1   and   2   and   1   and   2   and   Played like 1st measure

Presto

Dotted Eighth Notes

Repeat several times . (Try clapping the rhythm before playing.)

Count   1 - 2   1 - 2

Start and Stop

Stop the bow for each staccato note .

Joy To The World

GEORGE F. HANDEL

Orchestra Bass Part

In Key of D

Oh! Susanna

STEPHEN C. FOSTER

Accents (>)

Accents are procured by putting momentary pressure on the bow, causing a quick "bite" or "attack" of the string.

Playing in Second Position

To play in second position the hand is placed a half tone higher than first position.

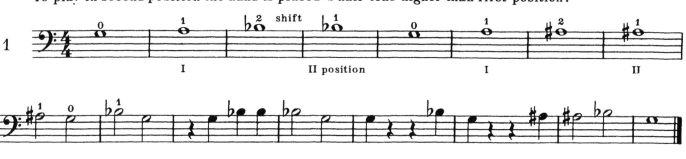

C Major Scale

Observe the Shift

Have you noticed that the half steps in any Major scale always come between the 3rd and 4th and 7th and 8th degrees of the scale?

Practice Shifting

Melody

Second Position on the D String

Name the notes before playing.

Is your 4th finger in tune? Test it with G open string

What scale is this?

Shifting

Melody

Allegro moderato

S.D.W.

Second Position on the A String

Name the notes before playing them.

Second Position on the E String

Crossing the Strings in Second Position

Etude

For review in half, first and second positions

S. D. W.

Playing Triplets

Choose your fingering carefully

Romance

S. D. W.

Pizzicato

(Or plucking the string with the finger)

The string is plucked with the index finger of the right hand about a foot from the end of the finger-board, while the bow hangs supported by the rest of the fingers. The thumb is pressed against the edge of the fingerboard to steady the hand. See illustration page 2.

Alternating Pizzicato and Bowing

Amaryllis Gavotte

KING LOUIS XIII

The Intermediate Position Between Second and Third*

(This position lies one-half tone higher than second position)

*The intermediate position indicated in this way $\frac{II}{III}$

42

A♭ Major and D♭ Major Scales Played in $\frac{II}{III}$ Intermediate Position

Always keep this position in mind when playing in these keys

Blue Bells of Scotland

SCOTCH AIR

Auld Lang Syne

Carry Me Back To Old Virginny

JAMES BLAND

The Loreley

FR. SILCHER

44

The Third Position

39587

March Cadet

S. D. W.

Count 1 - 2

Etude

S. D. W.

D Major Scale

Shifting Exercises

D Minor Scale

Russian Hymn

Reuben and Rachel

First practice separate bowing, then as marked.

Third Position (Continued)

Annie Laurie

LADY JOHN SCOTT

E MAJOR SCALE

Crossing the Strings in Third Position

Believe Me If All Those Endearing Young Charms

Moderato

The Third and Fourth Intermediate Position $\left(\begin{smallmatrix}III\\IV\end{smallmatrix}\right)$

B♭ Major Scale

Eb Major Scale

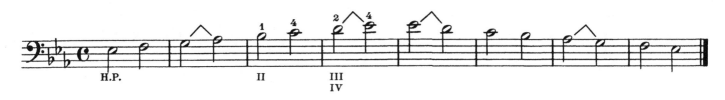

H.P.　　II　　III　　IV

Darling Nellie Grey

B. R. HANBY

Crossing the Strings in $\frac{III}{IV}$ Intermediate Position

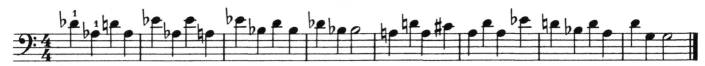

The Last Rose of Summer

FLOTOW

39587

III IV Intermediate Position (Continued)

Shifting

F MAJOR SCALE

Piece in Minor Key

Crossing the Strings in $\frac{III}{IV}$ Intermediate Position

Rocked in the Cradle of the Deep

JOSEPH P. KNIGHT

rit.

Tremolo

Tremolo is a quivering of the bow, executed in the middle of the bow, using a rapid wrist action.

Written

Played

or *trem.*

Written

Played

39587

Fourth Position

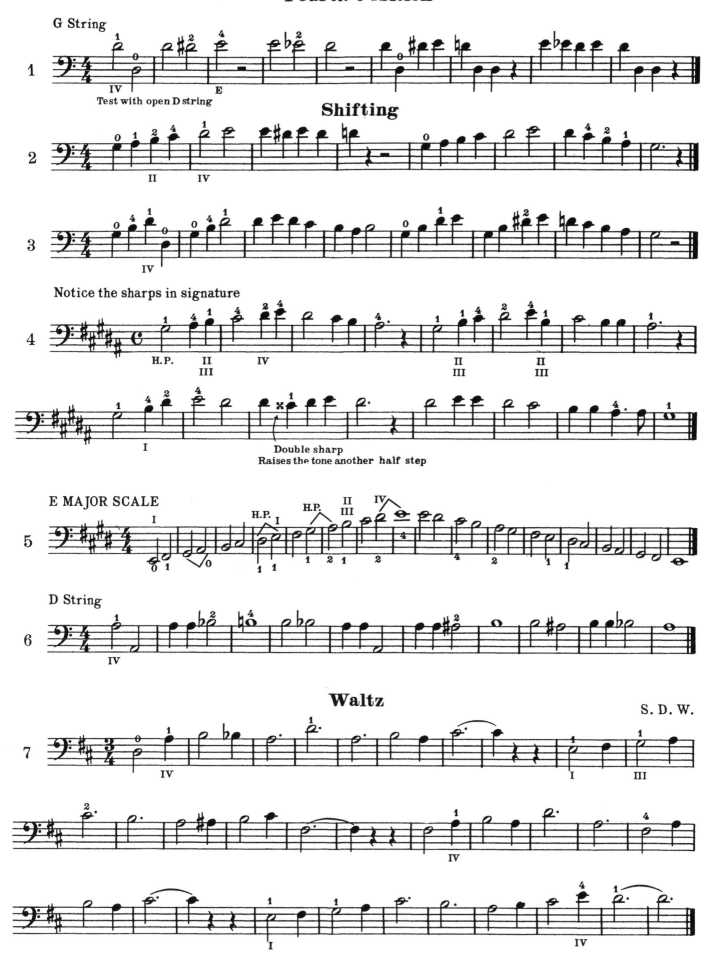

Fourth Position (Continued)

Practice Fingering as Marked

Tin Soldier Parade

S. D. W.

Grace note – Play very quickly

Fourth Position (Continued)

Andantino

EDWIN H. LEMARE

Crossing the Strings in Fourth Position

Where Has My Little Dog Gone

Allegro

German Song

Waltz Dorrell

S.D.W.

Fine

Vigorously

Smoothly, with long bows

D.C

Study of Intervals

Practice intervals carefully. They will give you a good understanding of the positions.

THIRDS

FOURTHS

FIFTHS

Intervals (Continued)

SIXTHS

SEVENTHS

OCTAVES

Harmonic (Touch the string lightly with the third finger only)

Learning the Trill

Also practice using other fingers on different notes and strings

Brahm's Lullaby
(Duet)

Arr. by R.C.W.

Silent Night

FRANZ GRUBER

39587

Peasant Song*

(Duet)

Moderato con moto

S. D. W.

---

* You can also play this piece with the Violas. See Rubanks' Elementary Viola Method Page 46.

REFERENCE CHART OF

The 1st, 2nd and 4th fingers are used to finger the notes on the String Bass. This fingering applies to all positions up to the sixth position. From the sixth position up, the 4th finger is no longer used— the 3rd finger taking its place. Beginning with the fifth position, the thumb moves toward the left side of the neck, while in the lower positions it is directly under the neck.

POSITIONS AND FINGERING

In the sixth and seventh intermediate position the thumb takes its place along the side of the fingerboard. Study this chart thoroughly so you will know the name of any note and fingering on sight, as well as the position.

Fourth Position (IV)	Fifth Position (V)	Fifth & Sixth Intermediate Position (V—VI)	Sixth Position (VI)	Sixth & Seventh Intermediate Position (VI—VII)	Seventh Position (VII)
D Double Sharp	E Sharp	F Sharp	F Double Sharp	G Sharp	G Double Sharp
E	F	G Flat	G	A Flat	A
A Double Sharp					

Third finger not used here.

Third finger not used on these strings in this high position.

E String not used in this position.

E String not used in this position.

SOLOS
FOR
STRINGS

AN INDISPENSABLE STRING INSTRUMENT COLLECTION FOR SOLO OR SECTIONAL UNISON PLAYING.

COMPILED AND ARRANGED BY

Harvey S. Whistler

FOR

VIOLIN SOLO (First Position)   CELLO SOLO (First Position)

VIOLA SOLO (First Position)   STRING BASS SOLO (First & Second Positions)

PIANO ACCOMPANIMENT

★

CONTENTS

		No.
ANDANTE—from Fifth Symphony	Tschaikowsky	12
ANDANTINO	Lemare	6
BARCAROLLE—from Tales of Hoffmann	Offenbach	5
DRINK TO ME ONLY WITH THINE EYES	Old English Ballad	7
EVENING STAR—from Tannhauser	Wagner	10
LARGO—from New World Symphony	Dvorak	1
LIEBESTRAUME	Liszt	9
MELODY IN F	Rubenstein	3
NOCTURNE	Von Blon	11
SWANEE RIVER	Stephen C. Foster	8
MERRY WIDOW WALTZ	Franz Lehar	2
VOLGA BOATMAN	Russian Folk Song	4